FOILED!

FOILED!

EASY, TASTY, TIN FOIL MEALS

JESSECA HALLOWS

FRONT TABLE BOOKS | AN IMPRINT OF CEDAR FORT, INC. | SPRINGVILLE, UTAH

ISBN 13: 978-1-4621-1841-0

Published by Front Table Books, an imprint of Cedar Fort, Inc.
2373 W. 700 S., Springville, UT 84663
Distributed by Cedar Fort, Inc., www.cedarfort.com

LIBRARY OF CONGRESS CATALOGING-IN-PUBLICATION DATA

Names: Hallows, Jesseca, 1987- author.
Title: Foiled! : easy, tasty tinfoil meals / Jesseca Hallows.
Description: Springville, Utah : Front Table Books, 2015. | Includes index.
Identifiers: LCCN 2015041234 | ISBN 9781462118410 (layflat binding : alk.
 paper)
Subjects: LCSH: Cooking. | Quick and easy cooking. | Aluminum foil. | LCGFT:
 Cookbooks.
Classification: LCC TX652 .H347 2015 | DDC 641.5/12--dc23
LC record available at http://lccn.loc.gov/2015041234

Cover and page design by M. Shaun McMurdie
Cover design © 2016 Cedar Fort, Inc.
Edited by Melissa J. Caldwell

Printed in China

10 9 8 7 6 5 4 3 2 1

Printed on acid-free paper

DEDICATION

To my husband, who always finds me a camping spot with a shower.

CONTENTS

ACKNOWLEDGMENTS

Mom—Thank you for spending countless days at the grocery store and letting me take over your kitchen for this endeavor. I could not have finished this without you.

Morgan and Dax—Thank you for being patient with me through the cooking process and eating more tin foil dinners than anyone thought possible. Your taste testing helped shape each recipe and I would be lost without you.

Special thanks to Harmons and Tillamook for their support!

INTRODUCTION

When I told my husband I wanted to write a camping cookbook I am pretty sure the look on his face was complete shock. Since he's known me, I haven't been too keen on the idea of temporary living in the great outdoors (this city girl loves running water!). The funny thing is, growing up I spent many weekends sleeping under the stars in California with my family. We loved the hikes, fishing, reading by the lake, and most of all the *food*. As the years have gone by I've stopped attending our family gatherings and those great memories slowly slipped out of my mind.

It wasn't until a dinner with friends that all of the nostalgia came flooding back. We decided to create a tin foil meal bar as an interactive dinner that would help as a little ice breaker. Everyone gathered around the kitchen counter adding their choice of ingredients building their dinner masterpieces. Since then, we have used this idea on several occasions as a quick and fun dinner party theme as well as our contribution for group camping trips. All of which gave me the great idea to bring a little of this happiness to my website.

Over the last three years, tin foil recipes have continued to climb the ranks in my recipe archives and claim their spot as the most popular. The idea of a meal that is quick to put together and cooks in the same container that it is served in was appealing to campers and home cooks alike. I started with the basic Hobo Dinner (hamburger and vegetables) and slowly watched as the recipe skyrocketed to my most viewed. I took ahold of the enthusiasm from my audience and started to create unique tin foil meals.

In this book you will find everything from breakfasts to desserts. Don't limit these meals to the open flame. If you are craving a little summer flavor, you can try cooking these on the grill or in the oven! My goal was to provide you with a fun list of new and different ideas that will make camping, or everyday cooking, even more delicious.

HELPFUL SUPPLIES

Over the years, I've discovered that some tools are essential to making a good tin foil meal. The following is a list of items I can't do without.

- *Heavy-duty foil*
- *Foil baking dishes (9 x 9 square muffin tin and 8-inch cake pan)*
- *Metal grate or campfire grill*
- *Nonstick cooking spray*
- *Oven mitt or fire glove*

When cooking straight on hot coals, it is always best to use heavy-duty foil. Most of the time I like to double up and have two thick layers protecting the food. Other items that are helpful are metal grates or a campfire grill and an oven mitt. We use a heavy-duty leather glove, which helps when we need to turn or pull our tin foil packets off the hot coals. This helps to avoid burning yourself and spoiling your camping fun.

The foil baking dishes can be found in the baking aisle next to the foil. Sometimes there are foil dishes in the pots and pans aisle too.

COOKING AT HOME, ON A BARBECUE GRILL, OR ON COALS

Tin foil meals are simply delicious when camping! But sometimes you don't have time to head for the woods. If you're hankering for some camping flavor without the mess, tin foil meals are the way to go. You can easily cook them in the oven, on the grill, or even on top of charcoals.

In oven: Preheat oven to 350 degrees. Make the tin foil packets as directed and then place in oven for 30-45 minutes. Each packet will take a different amount of time, so be sure to check on them at 30 minutes to determine how much longer to cook them. Pull the packets out once they're done, open them up, and enjoy!

On grill: Turn on grill and let it get to a nice hot temperature. Place packets directly on grill for 10-15 minutes. Flip packets over and grill another 10-15 minutes. Check to see if they're done. If not, cook for another 5-10 minutes. Pull the packets out once they're done, open them up, and enjoy!

On coals: Be sure to be in a well-ventilated area when you're using coals, like in a car port or on a driveway. Light 15-20 coals and let them burn until they're white (that's when they're perfect for baking). Place packets on top and cook for 15-20 minutes. Flip over and cook for another 15-20 minutes. Check to see if they're done. Once they are done, pull the packets out, open them up, and enjoy!

COOKING TIPS

Cooking tin foil dinners can be tricky, especially if you're cooking on coals or straight on the fire. Here are some tips that will make it a little easier.

- *Make sure your packets are sealed tightly.* Folding the top and edges verses bunching helps to create a solid cooking container.
- *Always use cooking spray.* There are a few recipes created in this book where I skipped this step and regretted it. Food sticking to the bottom of your packet is never fun.
- *Thinly slice your vegetables.* Potatoes and other thick vegetables can take a while to cook. Slicing or cutting them into smaller portions helps speed up the cooking time.
- *Rice and pasta need to be precooked before adding.* Make a large batch before you take off and store it in the cooler in large resealable bags.
- *Meat takes the longest to cook.* Make sure you keep the meat toward the outside of a packet.
- *Don't forget to heat your coals.* In order to get the right cooking temperature, you want your coals to have time to mature. I suggest letting them heat for at least half an hour before cooking.
- *If you are worried your dinner will be too dry, try adding in some water or ice cubes for a little added moisture.*

Try to remember that tin foil recipes are not exact. You will have to adjust the cooking times according to the heat level of your coals.

MAKE-AHEAD DISHES

I am a huge fan of make-ahead meals. The last thing I want to do when on vacation is to spend hours prepping and cleaning a meal. Most of these recipes have some prep work required before you take off for your adventures. Make sure you read the directions carefully before you get ready to make your recipe.

I've marked the recipes that have make-ahead items so it's easier for you to prep.

HOW TO FOLD A TIN FOIL PACKET

1 Start by cutting a piece of heavy-duty tin foil big enough to fit your meal. I recommend 12–18 inches long.

2 Generously mist your foil with nonstick cooking spray.

3 Layer your food directly in the center of your foil.

4 Bring the two longer edges together above the food. Fold the edges down twice, creating the top seal.

5 Press the side edges together and fold, creating a secure packet.

BREAKFAST

It's the most important meal of the day, even more so when you are out in the wilderness preparing for a busy day full of excursions. Make sure you start it right with one of these easy breakfasts!

BREAKFAST BURRITOS

This is one of our favorite camping breakfasts. All of the prep is done before you even leave the house, which means all you have to do in the morning is toss a foil-wrapped burrito right onto the warm coals and let it heat through!

MAKES 24 SMALL or 12 LARGE BURRITOS

INSTRUCTIONS

At Home

1. Cook the potatoes according to the package and brown the sausage in a large skillet. Set aside.

2. Crack all eggs into a giant bowl. Whisk in the sour cream, salt and pepper, and garlic powder.

3. Heat up a large skillet, and spray with nonstick spray.

4. Pour your eggs into the warm pan and cook, stirring occasionally, until fluffy and set, about 4 minutes.

5. In a smaller bowl, combine your peppers and onions with a small amount of oil. Sauté until onions are transparent and peppers are tender.

6. Combine the eggs, sausage, cheese, onion mixture, and potatoes in a large bowl. Mix to combine.

7. Warm the tortillas in the microwave. Working with one at a time, fill with ¼–½ cup of your egg mixture. Fold in the two sides and roll up tightly.

8. Wrap each burrito in tin foil and place into a resealable bag for easy storage.

At Camp

1. When you are ready to eat, toss the burritos on warm coals. Cook 10–15 minutes or until heated through, making sure to turn frequently.

INGREDIENTS

1 bag **frozen potatoes** (the style is up to you)

1½ lb. **sausage**

18 **eggs**

¼–½ cup **sour cream**

1 tsp. **salt**

¼ tsp. **pepper**

¼ tsp. **garlic powder**

peppers & onions, chopped (optional)

16 oz. **cheese** (use your favorite kind)

24 **small tortillas** or 12 **large tortillas**

foil

TIPS

• *Adjust the seasonings according to your tastes. You might want more or less salt and garlic powder.*

• *Use the same skillet you cooked your sausage in to cook your eggs for added flavor. Lightly mist with cooking spray before you pour the eggs in to keep them from sticking.*

• *Freeze burritos to help keep them cool until ready to eat.*

EGG SANDWICH

I love this recipe because it is simple and a camping classic. Make them ahead or while out at the campsite.

SERVES 6

INSTRUCTIONS

At Home

1. Toast your English muffins or bagels and spread with butter. Set aside.

2. Crack 1 egg over a heated skillet that has been misted with cooking spray or spread with butter. Sprinkle with salt and pepper according to your tastes. Cook for 1 minute or until the whites start to set. Gently break the yolk and flip your egg and cook for 1 additional minute. Top with cheese and place on the bottom half of your prepared bread.

3. Top your egg with 2 slices of ham and sandwich with the top slice of bread. Wrap tightly in foil and place in resealable bag for easy storage.

At Camp

1. When ready to eat, place sandwiches on a grate over heated coals. Cook up to 10 minutes or until heated through.

INGREDIENTS

6 **English muffins** or **bagels**

butter, softened

6 **eggs**

6 slices **cheddar**

12 slices of **ham**

salt and **pepper**

TIPS

• *Substitute ham for 3 slices of bacon, 2 slices Canadian bacon, or your favorite breakfast meat.*

• *Typically, I make 3 eggs at one time. Make sure you don't do too many at once to avoid burning.*

EGG SCRAMBLE

This easy breakfast scramble combines all of your favorite breakfast foods into 1 bowl and is ready in under 15 minutes! It is a great way to use up leftover veggies or cooked bacon from previous meals.

SERVES 2

INSTRUCTIONS

1. Layer two sheets of heavy-duty foil and fold the edges up to form a bowl with enough edges to close. Mist with nonstick spray.
2. Whisk together the eggs, milk, salt, and pepper. Pour into your prepared bowl. Sprinkle with the cooked bacon, cheese, green onion, and veggies.
3. Fold the edges of the foil, making sure to seal tightly.
4. Place on hot coals and cook 10–15 minutes. We like to use a fire grill because we aren't turning anything over, but direct coals work just as well. Just keep a close eye to avoid burning.

INGREDIENTS

4 **eggs**

2 Tbsp. **milk**

⅛ tsp. **salt**

⅛ tsp. **pepper**

4 slices cooked **bacon**, chopped

½ cup shredded **cheddar cheese**

1 chopped **green onion**

diced **veggies** of choice

TIPS
• *Switch up the ingredients to customize the flavors. Instead of bacon, try sausage or diced ham or a sweet onion in place of the green.*

MAPLE BACON **ROLLS**

With just a few adjustments, a canned cinnamon roll can be turned gourmet! This is a great way to use up leftover bacon from a previous breakfast, or you can cook a large batch and save some for the next day. Using the orange isn't a new method and helps keep each roll from burning.

SERVES 2

INSTRUCTIONS

At Home

1. Before you leave for your trip, you'll want to whisk together the powdered sugar, melted butter, and syrup in a small bowl. Add milk a little at a time until a good consistency is reached. Store the frosting in a resealable bag.

At Camp

1. When ready to eat, slice the oranges in half. Scoop the fruit out, keeping the peel intact. Set aside.

2. Open your can of cinnamon rolls. Unroll 1 cinnamon roll carefully. Place a strip of bacon inside and roll it back up. Place in an intact orange peel. Cover with another orange peel and wrap tightly in foil.

3. Repeat with the remaining rolls.

4. Cook on warm coals 10–12 minutes or until cooked through, flipping at least once.

5. Drizzle with your maple frosting or the frosting in the cinnamon roll package.

INGREDIENTS

½ cup **powdered sugar**

1 Tbsp. **melted butter**

4 tsp. **maple syrup**

1 tsp. **milk** (maybe less)

5 **oranges**

1 can **cinnamon rolls**

5 strips slightly cooked **bacon**

TIP
• *We buy fully cooked bacon that is located in the meat aisle of the grocery store. It saves on the step of cooking the bacon and is easy to prepare alongside every breakfast.*

EGG IN **A** HOLE

I remember this breakfast growing up. The classic Egg in a Hole starts with a slice of bread. Add an egg and some crushed bacon and you've got a quick breakfast bake ready to go!

SERVES 4

INSTRUCTIONS

1. Layer 2 pieces of heavy-duty foil and lightly mist with cooking spray.

2. Take 1 slice of bread and spread with softened butter. Using a cup, cut a circle directly in the center of the bread. Place bread butter-side down on your foil.

3. Crack your egg directly into the circle of the bread. Sprinkle with salt and pepper, cheese, and 1 slice of crumbled bacon. Repeat with remaining eggs.

4. Fold your tin foil over your egg and bread, creating a tent. Seal closed and place onto a grate over warmed coals. Cook 5–10 minutes or until whites are firm.

INGREDIENTS

4 slices Harmons 7-Grain Artisan **Bread**

softened **butter**

4 **eggs**

4 slices **bacon**, cooked and crumbled

¼ cup **shredded cheese**

1 tsp. both **salt** and **pepper**

TIPS
- *We love 7-grain bread but you can swap this for any type of bread. Use a thicker variety to make sure you have room for the egg.*

- *Grab fresh cheese that hasn't been grated for the best melt.*

WARM GRANOLA **BOWL**

This granola recipe is a staple in our home and when we are out camping. It's easy to prepare and easy to customize for a fun breakfast or snack.

SERVES 4

INSTRUCTIONS

1. Layer two heavy-duty sheets of foil and generously coat with nonstick spray. Repeat so you have 2 foil packets prepared.

2. In a large bowl, combine the oats, brown sugar, salt, and cinnamon.

3. In a separate bowl, stir the oil, honey, syrup, and vanilla together. Pour over your oats and stir until coated.

4. Divide your oats between the 2 prepared sheets of foil.

5. Fold edges to create a closed packet and place on a grill grate over hot coals.

6. Cook 12–15 minutes, gently shaking the granola every few minutes to help with even cooking.

7. Remove from the heat, stir, and add in dried fruit or additional ingredients.

INGREDIENTS

4 cups **rolled oats**

½ cup **brown sugar**

¼ tsp. **salt**

¼ tsp. **cinnamon**

⅓ cup **oil**

¼ cup **honey**

1 Tbsp. **maple syrup**

4 tsp. **pure vanilla extract**

dried fruit

TIP

• *Some add-in ingredients we enjoy are dried bananas, dried blueberries, fresh fruit, toasted coconut, pecans, walnuts, and almonds.*

TIN FOIL OATMEAL

This breakfast has to be the easiest in the book. Stir all of the ingredients together and cook for only 5 minutes. Stir in fruit, nuts, or coconut for an even more satisfying meal.

SERVES 4

INSTRUCTIONS

1. Combine the oats, brown sugar, and salt in a large ziplock bag. Seal and give a good shake to combine the ingredients.

2. Measure ¾ cup of your oat mixture into a tin foil bowl. Pour 1 cup of water into the mix. Place on a grate over warm coals and let cook 5 minutes.

3. Stir in your favorite add-in ingredients and enjoy!

INGREDIENTS

3 cups **quick cook oats**

¼ cup **brown sugar**

½ tsp. **salt**

water

ADD-IN OPTIONS:

blueberries

bananas

diced apples

chocolate chips

coconut

pecans

honey

TIPS
• *You can mix the dry ingredients up to two weeks before your trip.*

• *Substitute instant oatmeal packets for the dried oat mixture for an even easier meal. Decrease the water amount to ⅔ cup.*

MAIN DISHES

Camping food should be simple and delicious. These recipes nail that description on the head. They are quick to whip up and leave virtually no mess. Some prep is done before you leave the house, which guarantees a stress-free trip!

CHICKEN STACK

Chicken topped with a sweet pineapple lying on a bed of rice, this meal is unique and filling.

SERVES 4

INSTRUCTIONS

1. Combine the chicken and the ¼ cup of teriyaki sauce in a ziplock plastic bag. Keep refrigerated or in a cooler for at least 2 hours.

2. Create 4 rectangles of heavy-duty foil.

3. Spray your containers with cooking spray and divide the rice between them evenly. Top with chicken and remaining ingredients. Fold up the sides to create your packet.

4. Place your packets onto prepared coals. Cook for 30 minutes making sure to turn a few times for even cooking.

INGREDIENTS

1½ lb. **chicken**, chopped or sliced

¼ cup **teriyaki sauce**, plus more for topping

2 cups **cooked rice**

red and green peppers, sliced

onions, sliced

broccoli

pineapple

peas

TIP
• *Add vegetables based on your preferred tastes.*

BRUSCHETTA CHICKEN

This bruschetta chicken is packed with color and flavor. Perfect for large groups or single servings.

SERVES 2

INSTRUCTIONS

1. Combine the chicken and 2 tablespoons of the dressing in a ziplock plastic bag. Keep refrigerated or in a cooler for at least 2 hours.

2. Create 2 foil packets. Lightly mist with cooking spray. Place one chicken breast in each foil packet. Fold and place on warm coals. Cook 10 minutes, turning once halfway through.

3. While your chicken is cooking, stir together the tomato, cheeses, basil, and remaining tablespoon of dressing. Carefully open your packets and divide the bruschetta between the two. Close and return to the warm coals.

4. Cook an additional 8–10 minutes, or until the chicken reaches 160 degrees.

INGREDIENTS

2 small **chicken breasts**

3 Tbsp. **sun-dried tomato salad dressing**, divided

1 large **tomato**, chopped

¼ cup shredded **mozzarella**

1 Tbsp. **shredded parmesan**

3 Tbsp. chopped **basil**

RANCH CHICKEN

An entire meal in one packet. This ranch chicken is loaded with flavor and paired with red potatoes and vegetables.

SERVES 4

INSTRUCTIONS

1. Lay 4 sheets of heavy-duty foil out for 4 packets. Coat each with nonstick spray.

2. Combine the sour cream with the ranch packet and the water. Divide into two bowls.

3. Stir the potatoes, carrots, and green beans into one of the bowls of ranch. Divide evenly between your 4 foil packets.

4. Dip the chicken into the remaining ranch bowl and then into the bread crumbs. Place 1 breast onto each vegetable pile.

5. Fold the sides of the packet, closing them tightly. Place on hot coals and cook for 10 minutes. Turn and cook 15 minutes more or until the chicken temperature reaches 160 degrees.

INGREDIENTS

1 cup **sour cream**

1 dry packet **ranch dressing mix**

2 Tbsp. **water**

2 cups thinly sliced **red potatoes**

1 cup sliced **small carrots**

1 cup **green beans**

4 **chicken breasts**

½ cup **bread crumbs**

SOUTHWESTERN CHICKEN PACKETS

Quick, easy, and delicious are the three words I would use to describe this dish. All of the flavors blend together to form the perfect southwestern meal. Garnish with sour cream, guacamole, and cilantro on top of warm tortillas!

SERVES 2

INSTRUCTIONS

1. Pull off 4 sheets of heavy-duty tin foil (8–10 inches) and layer to create 2 packets. Lightly mist with cooking spray.

2. Stir together the corn, black beans, and cumin. Divide between the 2 foil packets. Season the chicken with salt and pepper. Place 1 on each packet. Top with pico de gallo and cheese.

3. Fold up the sides of the foil and seal tightly. Cook on hot coals for 30 minutes or until chicken is cooked through, making sure to carefully turn 2 or 3 times to prevent burning.

4. Top with fresh cilantro, sour cream, and guacamole before serving.

INGREDIENTS

1 cup fresh or frozen **corn**

1 cup **canned black beans**, drained and rinsed

½ tsp. **cumin**

2 **chicken breasts**

salt and **pepper** to taste

½ cup **pico de gallo** or **salsa**

1 cup **pepper jack cheese**

cilantro, to garnish

sour cream (optional)

guacamole (optional)

TIP
• *Not a pepper jack fan? Use a cheddar or Taco blend cheese.*

BBQ CHICKEN

The beauty about chicken tin foil meals is the endless possibilities. This barbecue version is simple and pairs well with grilled veggies or corn bread!

SERVES 2

INSTRUCTIONS

1. Coat 2 sheets of foil with nonstick spray. Spread 2 tablespoons of barbecue sauce in the middle of each sheet.

2. Divide the potatoes between each foil packet. Spread evenly. Sprinkle with salt and pepper.

3. Top the potatoes with 1 chicken breast each. Spread 2 tablespoons sauce on each breast. Sprinkle with the sliced onion.

4. Fold the sides of the foil creating your closed packet. Place on warm coals and cook 20 minutes, turning once halfway through. Chicken is done when its juices run clear and it reaches an internal temperature of 160 degrees.

INGREDIENTS

½ cup **barbecue sauce**, divided

1 cup thinly sliced **golden potatoes**

salt and **pepper**

2 **chicken breasts**

¼ cup sliced **onion**

SWEET AND **SOUR** CHICKEN

This sweet and sour chicken is a fun twist to camping favorites. Try adding a little chopped onion for added crunch and flavor.

SERVES 2

INSTRUCTIONS

1. Create 2 rectangles of heavy-duty foil. Fold up the sides creating a 1-inch rim.

2. Spray your containers with cooking spray and divide the rice between them.

3. Toss your chicken in the sweet and sour sauce. Divide it over the rice.

4. Sprinkle the remaining ingredients over the chicken. Fold the edges of the foil together to create your packets.

5. Place your packets onto a grate over prepared coals. Cook for 30 minutes, making sure to turn a few times for even cooking.

INGREDIENTS

1½ cups **cooked rice**

2 **chicken breasts**, chopped

½ cup **sweet and sour sauce**, plus more for topping

½ each **red and green pepper**, cubed

1 can **diced pineapple**

CHICKEN FAJITAS

Warm tortillas filled with grilled chicken, peppers, and fresh pico de gallo.

SERVES 4

INSTRUCTIONS

1. Create 4 rectangles of heavy-duty foil. Fold up the sides creating a 1-inch rim.

2. Spray your containers with cooking spray and divide the rice between them evenly. Top with remaining ingredients, except tortillas. Make sure you evenly distribute the salsa and use more if necessary.

3. Fold up the sides to create your packets.

4. Place your packets onto prepared coals. Cook for 20–30 minutes, making sure to turn a few times.

5. Eat with the tortillas.

INGREDIENTS

2 cups cooked **white rice**

taco seasoning

1 lb. **chicken breasts**, chopped

1 **green pepper**, sliced

1 **red pepper**, sliced

½ **onion**, sliced

½ cup **salsa**

cheese, to taste

8 **tortillas**

TIPS
• *Top with fresh guacamole or pico de gallo from Harmons or made at home.*

PARMESAN CHICKEN DINNER

This meal requires a little bit of prep before you leave. Cook the spaghetti noodles at home and store in a big plastic container or bag.

SERVES 6

INSTRUCTIONS

At Home

1. Cook spaghetti noodles until they are al dente. Store in a big plastic container or bag.

At Camp

1. Coat 2 sheets of foil with nonstick spray.
2. Whisk together the olive oil, garlic, and salt and pepper. Place in a shallow bowl.
3. Stir the parmesan and bread crumbs together and spread onto a paper plate.
4. Spread ¼ cup spaghetti sauce onto each prepared sheet of foil. Divide the spaghetti between the foil sheets. Spread an additional ½ cup sauce over the noodles.
5. Dip the chicken into the oil mixture followed by the bread crumb mixture until completely covered. Place over the noodles.
6. Fold the edges of your foil packet to seal closed. Cook on warm coals for 20–30 minutes, making sure to turn a few times. Chicken is done when juices run clear and reaches an internal temperature of 160 degrees. Use extra spaghetti sauce as topping, if desired.

INGREDIENTS

3 cups **spaghetti**

1 Tbsp. **olive oil**

1 clove **garlic**

salt and **pepper**

⅓ cup finely **shredded parmesan**

1 cup **Italian bread crumbs**

2 cups **spaghetti sauce**

2 **chicken breasts**

TIP

• *Serve additional sauce over the top of your chicken.*

CLASSIC HOBO DINNER

Meat, potatoes, cream soup, and lots of veggies are what you'll find in this filling meal. Hobo dinners are the original tin foil camping meal.

SERVES 4

INSTRUCTIONS

1. Prep 4 sheets of foil with nonstick spray.

2. Spread a small amount of cream soup on the bottom of each piece of foil.

3. Divide the potatoes evenly between the sheets of foil, placing evenly over the soup.

4. Create 4 patties, ¼ pound each, with your ground beef. Place on top of your potatoes.

5. Fill each packet with the green beans, carrots, and onions. Season with salt and pepper. Spoon more soup over the entire dish. Fold foil over on each packet and seal well.

6. Place the packets on warmed coals. Cook 45–60 minutes or until meat is cooked through, making sure to turn frequently.

INGREDIENTS

1–2 cans **cream of chicken soup**

1½ cups thinly sliced **golden potatoes**

1 lb. **ground beef**

½ cup **fresh green beans**

½ cup chopped **baby carrots**

½ cup **onion** slices

salt and **pepper** to taste

TIPS
• *You can use any creamed soup with this recipe. Cheddar or cream of mushroom are two of our favorites.*

• *Switch up the vegetables for even more flavor options.*

ITALIAN SAUSAGE

This dish is like a grown-up version of a hot dog. Italian sausage paired with a fennel salt is a mouthwatering combination.

SERVES 4

INSTRUCTIONS

1. Start by dicing your potatoes into bite-sized chunks.

2. Create 4 rectangles of heavy-duty foil. Fold up the sides, creating a 1-inch rim.

3. Spray your containers with cooking spray and divide the potatoes between them evenly. Top with the sausage links and green beans. I like to slice the sausage beforehand, but you can leave it whole as well. Lightly drizzle your meal with olive oil and sprinkle with seasonings. Fold up the sides to create your packet.

4. Place your packets onto prepared coals. Cook for 30 minutes, making sure to turn a few times for even cooking.

INGREDIENTS

8 **red potatoes**, washed

4 **Italian sausage links**, uncooked

1 cup **fresh green beans**, ends cut

olive oil

fennel salt (or **salt** and **pepper**)

TIP
• *Like most tin foil recipes, this one is easily adaptable. Swap the green beans for your other favorite veggies.*

CHILI CHEESE **DOG**

My sons love this recipe! Plus, it's easy for me to whip up. Chili dogs are messy, which means they are ideal for outdoor eating.

SERVES 8

INSTRUCTIONS

1. Place hot dogs in buns and place in a square foil pan.

2. Top each dog with the chili, shredded cheese, and onions. Cover the pan with heavy-duty foil.

3. Place your container on a grate over heated coals and cook 10–15 minutes or until cheese is melted and chili is warm.

4. Top with mustard and ketchup.

INGREDIENTS

8 all-beef **hot dogs**

8 **hot dog buns**

2 (15-oz.) cans **chili with beans**

1–2 cups shredded **cheddar cheese**

¼ cup chopped **onion**

mustard and **ketchup**

TIPS

• *Cook the hot dogs beforehand on sticks over the flame of the fire for a more crisp texture.*

• *This recipe gives the buns a slight toasted taste. If you want soft buns, leave them out during the heating process and fill after the rest of the ingredients are heated.*

MEATLOAF

While not something you typically serve while enjoying the great outdoors, this meatloaf can be made ahead of time for an easy meal or mixed up in 1 bowl in under 15 minutes.

SERVES 6–8, DEPENDING ON THE SIZE OF THE LOAVES

INSTRUCTIONS

At Home

1. Mix the ground beef, egg, onion, milk, bread crumbs, salt, and pepper in a large bowl. Store the mixture in a large resealable bag.

At Camp

1. When you are ready to cook, prep 8 sheets of foil with nonstick cooking spray.

2. Whisk together the brown sugar, mustard, and ketchup. Spread 1–2 tablespoons in the middle of each sheet of foil.

3. Divide your meat mixture into 8 portions. Form into mini loaves and place 1 on each packet. Spoon the remaining ketchup mixture over all of the loaves.

4. Divide the potatoes and carrots between the packets. Fold and seal edges.

5. Cook on warm coals 20–30 minutes or until meat is cooked through.

INGREDIENTS

1½ lb. **ground beef**

1 **egg**

1 cup finely chopped **onion**

1 cup **milk**

1 cup **Italian bread crumbs**

½ tsp. **salt**

¼ tsp. **pepper**

2 Tbsp. **brown sugar**

2 Tbsp. **mustard**

⅓ cup **ketchup**

2 cups thinly sliced **potatoes**

2 cups sliced **baby carrots**

TIPS

• *Sauté the onions before adding if you aren't looking for a crunchy texture.*

• *Save leftovers for meatloaf sandwiches. Place pieces of meatloaf on 2 slices of bread for a quick lunch.*

MEATBALL SANDWICH

I like to keep my camping food as simple as possible. This recipe uses frozen meatballs for a quick and easy meal.

SERVES 6

INSTRUCTIONS

1. Prepare 6 sheets of tin foil by coating with nonstick cooking spray.

2. Spread 2 tablespoons of pasta sauce on each piece of foil. Top with 5–6 meatballs. Smother meatballs in additional pasta sauce and a slice of provolone cheese.

3. Fold edges of each packet together and seal. Cook on warmed coals 15–20 minutes or until heated through.

4. Spoon warm meatballs into hoagies and enjoy.

INGREDIENTS

1 container your favorite **pasta sauce**

1 pkg. **frozen meatballs**

6 slices **provolone cheese**

6 **hoagies**, sliced

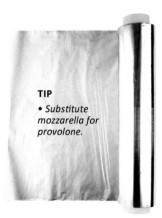

TIP
• *Substitute mozzarella for provolone.*

STUFFED PEPPERS

The peppers create an edible serving dish in this fun campfire recipe.

SERVES 4

INSTRUCTIONS

1. Mist 4 sheets of foil with cooking spray. Slice your peppers in half. Clean out the seeds and the membrane. Place each half pepper on a piece of foil.

2. Combine the yolk, onion, bread crumbs, garlic powder, Italian seasoning, onion powder, salt, pepper, rice, cooked sausage, and ½ cup marinara sauce. Spoon into your peppers and lightly spray the tops with cooking spray.

3. Fold the edges together to form a packet and place on a grate over warmed coals. Cook 20–25 minutes or until heated through.

4. Pour remaining marinara over the top before serving.

INGREDIENTS

2 **green** or **red peppers**

1 **egg yolk**

½ cup finely diced **onion**

¼ cup **bread crumbs**

1 tsp. **garlic powder**

1 Tbsp. **Italian seasoning**

¾ tsp. **onion powder**

¼ tsp. **salt**

⅛ tsp. **pepper**

1½ cups **cooked rice**

1 lb. cooked **Italian sausage**

1½ cups **marinara sauce**

TIP

• *Cook your sausage before you leave for your trip. Packet in a ziplock plastic bag in your cooler until ready to use. Just make sure you keep the temperature in the cooler cold enough to store meat.*

PHILLY CHEESESTEAK

I grew up with a similar version of this recipe making an appearance at our campouts. My dad would make this meal especially for me, and it's still one of my all-time favorites.

SERVES 4

INSTRUCTIONS

1. Prepare 4 sheets of tin foil with nonstick spray.

2. Spread the onions, mushrooms, and peppers onto your prepared sheets of foil. Top with your thinly sliced steak and season generously with salt and pepper. Top each with one slice of cheese.

3. Fold the edges of your foil up, creating a sealed packet. Cook on warm coals 15–20 minutes, flipping once halfway through.

4. Spread a thin layer of mayonnaise on your rolls.

5. Carefully open your packet and spoon the mixture into your prepared hoagie.

INGREDIENTS

1 **onion**, sliced

¾ cup sliced **mushrooms**

1 **green pepper**, sliced

1 lb. **sirloin steak**, thinly sliced

salt and **pepper** to taste

4 slices **provolone cheese**

mayonnaise, to taste

4 **hoagie rolls**, sliced

TIPS
• *Have the wonderful people behind the Harmons grocery counter slice your steak for you. They get it thin and save you prep time!*

• *Use steak seasoning in place of the salt and pepper for added flavor.*

CAMPFIRE TACOS

You shouldn't miss out on taco Tuesday just because you're enjoying the great outdoors!

SERVES 4

INSTRUCTIONS

1. Prep 4 sheets of foil with nonstick spray. Fold the edges up slightly, creating a bowl.

2. Divide the beef between the 4 dishes. Top with beans and corn. Pour ¼ cup of water in each packet followed by 1½ teaspoon taco seasoning. Fold edges to seal packet.

3. Cook on warm coals 10 minutes or until most of the water is dissolved and meat is heated through.

4. Serve inside tortillas and topped with your favorite toppings.

INGREDIENTS

1 lb. **ground beef**, cooked

1 can **black beans**, rinsed

1 can **corn**, drained

1 cup **water**, divided

1 packet **taco seasoning**

8 **corn tortillas** or 4 **flour tortillas**

TOPPINGS

2 cups **shredded cheese**

fresh **pico de gallo**

guacamole

sour cream

chopped **lettuce**

CRESCENT-WRAPPED HOT DOGS

This recipe is an easy, last-minute meal idea. Just 2 ingredients means dinner is on the table in no time.

SERVES 6

INSTRUCTIONS

1. Unroll the dough on a clean surface.

2. Roll one hot dog in each individual crescent.

3. Place each dog on a lightly sprayed piece of tin foil. Wrap tightly.

4. Place hot dogs on grate over heated coals. Cook 12–15 minutes or until dough is cooked through.

INGREDIENTS

1 can **crescent dough**

8 **hot dogs**

GARLIC SHRIMP

Shrimp lovers rejoice! This recipe is simple to whip up and delicious with a little cooked pasta tossed in olive oil.

SERVES 4

INSTRUCTIONS

1. Combine the butter, lemon juice, garlic, parsley, and pepper in a resealable bag.

2. Add shrimp to the bag. Seal and gently shake to coat. Place in a cooler for 1 hour.

3. Prepare 3 sheets of heavy-duty foil by coating in nonstick spray. Divide your shrimp among them. Fold up the sides to create your packets.

4. Place on warm coals and cook 3 minutes on each side or until the shrimp is pink in color.

INGREDIENTS

2 Tbsp. **butter**, melted

2 Tbsp. fresh **lemon juice**

1½ tsp. minced **garlic**

4 tsp. fresh chopped **parsley**

¼ tsp. **pepper**, more or less to taste

¾ lb. **shrimp**, peeled and deveined

cooked **pasta** (optional)

parmesan cheese (optional)

TIPS
• *Serve with pasta and sprinkled parmesan cheese.*

• *Great with the onion bread (see page 90).*

COCONUT LIME HALIBUT

This recipe works great with any white fish (think halibut or cod). Cooking with the coconut milk right in the packet makes for a fun steaming effect, and the lime adds an amazing citrus zing. We have made this in the oven on a regular basis and love it more every time!

SERVES 2

INSTRUCTIONS

1. Cut 4 sheets of heavy-duty tin foil (8–10 inches) and layer to create 2 packets. Lightly mist with cooking spray.

2. Combine the onion, garlic, zucchini, and squash in a large bowl. Sprinkle with the salt and pepper. Drizzle with olive oil and toss to coat. Divide between your 2 foil sheets.

3. Fold up the edges, creating a slight bowl. Whisk the coconut milk, lime zest, and lime juice in a small bowl. Pour over the vegetables.

4. In each packet, place the fish on top of the vegetable coconut mixture. Season with salt and pepper.

5. Fold up the sides of the foil and seal each packet tightly. Place on the heated campfire grate with the fish on top. Cook 10 minutes, carefully flip, and continue to cook 10 minutes more.

INGREDIENTS

½ cup sliced **red onion**

1 tsp. **garlic**

½ cup sliced **zucchini**

½ cup sliced **yellow summer squash**

salt and **pepper**, to taste

1 Tbsp. **olive oil**

½ cup **coconut milk**

1 tsp. **lime zest**

juice of 1 **lime**

8 oz. **halibut**, divided in half

TIP
• *Use in season vegetables or family favorites instead of the zucchini and squash.*

COCONUT SHRIMP

This shrimp has a slight kick to it from the jalapeño, which is toned down with the sweetness of coconut.

SERVES 2–4

INSTRUCTIONS

At Home

1. Combine everything except shrimp in a food processor. Pulse until smooth and transfer to a resealable container.

At Camp

1. Two hours before eating, stir the shrimp into your marinade. Return to a cooler to rest.
2. Prep 3 sheets of foil with nonstick spray.
3. Divide your shrimp between the prepared sheets of foil. Fold up the sides to create packets.
4. Place on warm coals and cook 3 minutes on each side or until the shrimp is pink in color.

INGREDIENTS

1 **jalapeño**, sliced and seeded

3 Tbsp. **lime juice**

2 tsp. **lime zest**

1 Tbsp. **coconut milk**

1 clove **garlic**

2 Tbsp. chopped **cilantro**

3 Tbsp. finely **shredded coconut**

2 Tbsp. **olive oil**

1½ tsp. **soy sauce**

¾ lb. **shrimp**, peeled and deveined

CHEESE ENCHILADAS

I love simple recipes that taste delicious when camping, and this recipe is just that. Add chicken or cooked ground beef if desired, but it's great all on its own.

SERVES 10

INSTRUCTIONS

1. Stir together the cheeses, chilies, sour cream, parsley, and salt and pepper.

2. Divide the filling between your tortillas. Roll each tortilla tightly and place in two 9-inch foil baking dishes.

3. Pour 1 cup sauce over each set of enchiladas. Cover with heavy-duty foil and place on a grate over heated coals. Cook 20 minutes or until heated through and cheese melted.

INGREDIENTS

4 cups **pepper jack** or **monterey jack cheese**

2½ cups **cheddar cheese**

1 (4-oz.) can **green chilies**

1 cup **sour cream**

¼ cup chopped **parsley**

½ tsp. both **salt** and **pepper**

10 medium **flour tortillas**

2 cups **enchilada sauce**

ANY ADDITIONAL TOPPINGS

tomatoes

pico de gallo

olives

corn

HOT HAM-AND-CHEESE **SANDWICH**

These sandwiches are perfect for a quick lunch or dinner. Serve with a side of chips or fresh veggies.

SERVES 6

INSTRUCTIONS

1. Prepare 6 sheets of foil.
2. Build your sandwiches by dividing the ham between the 12 rolls with 1 slice of cheese on each. Place 2 sandwiches onto each piece of foil.
3. Whisk together the butter, Dijon, onion, and brown sugar. Pour evenly over the sandwiches.
4. Fold the sides of each packet up and seal closed. Place on warm coals, turn frequently, and cook 10–15 minutes or until cheese is melted and bread is lightly toasted.

INGREDIENTS

1 lb. **ham slices**

12 **Hawaiian rolls**

12 slices **Swiss** or **provolone cheese**

½ cup **butter,** melted

1½ Tbsp. **Dijon mustard**

1 Tbsp. **dried onion**

1 Tbsp. **brown sugar**

HAWAIIAN HAM

Pineapple and ham create a salty-sweet combination in this fun dinner.

SERVES 4

INSTRUCTIONS

1. Create 4 rectangles of heavy-duty foil. Fold up the sides creating a 1-inch rim.

2. Spray your containers with cooking spray and divide the rice between them evenly. Chop your ham steak into cubes. Top packets with the ham and your remaining ingredients. Fold up the sides to create your packet.

3. Place your packets onto prepared coals. Cook for 15 minutes or until heated through, making sure to turn a few times for even cooking.

INGREDIENTS

2 cups **cooked rice**

1 **ham steak**

1 can sliced **pineapple**

¼ cup sliced **red peppers**

¼ cup sliced **green peppers**

¼ cup **soy sauce**

TIP
• *This recipe is a great one to play around with. Add your favorite veggies for fresh flavors.*

LOADED BAKED POTATOES

These potatoes are great on their own or as a filling side dish. Set up a topping bar and let everyone add their favorites!

SERVES 2

INSTRUCTIONS

1. Wash your potatoes well. Chop into 1-inch squares and divide between 2 sheets of foil that have been lightly coated with cooking spray.

2. Sprinkle with butter, bacon, and salt and pepper. Fold up the edges of the foil and create a tightly sealed packet. Place on warm coals and cook for 30 minutes or until potatoes are soft.

3. Top with cheddar, sour cream, and green onions when ready to serve.

INGREDIENTS

2 large baking **potatoes**

4 Tbsp. **butter**, divided

4 slices **bacon**, slightly cooked and chopped

salt and **pepper**, to taste

TOPPINGS

1 cup **cheddar cheese**

green onions

sour cream

TIP

• *For a more filling meal, try topping with chili and cheese or even broccoli and cheese.*

CHEESY BROCCOLI AND RICE

Meatless Monday has never tasted so good. Make this cheesy broccoli dish as written or add in some chopped chicken.

SERVES 4

INSTRUCTIONS

1. Cut 4 rectangles from heavy-duty foil. Spray them with cooking spray.

2. Stir all ingredients together in a large bowl. Divide between your prepared foil sheets. Fold up the edges sealing your packet closed.

3. Place your packets onto prepared coals. Cook for 20 minutes or until heated through, making sure to turn a few times for even cooking.

INGREDIENTS

1½ cups chopped **broccoli**

2 cans **cream of cheddar cheese soup**

2 cups **cooked rice**

1 tsp. **onion powder**

½ tsp. **salt**

¼ tsp. **pepper**

TIP
• *Substitute cream of chicken or mushroom for one or both of the canned soups.*

CHEESY HAM AND POTATOES

We love this easy and filling meal. The combination of ham and potatoes is a classic and tastes great smothered in cheese!

SERVES 4

INSTRUCTIONS

1. Create 4 rectangles of heavy-duty foil. Spray them with cooking spray.

2. Stir the first 6 ingredients together in a large bowl. Divide evenly between the 4 packets. Sprinkle cheese in each one.

3. Fold up the sides to create your packet.

4. Place your packets onto prepared coals. Cook for 1 hour or until the potatoes are soft, making sure to turn a few times for even cooking.

INGREDIENTS

1 **ham steak**, cubed

3 large **potatoes**, cubed

½ cup finely diced **onions**

½ tsp. **seasoned salt**

¼ tsp. **pepper**

¼ cup **butter**, melted

1 cup **cheddar cheese**

TIPS

• *Try swapping the ham steak for bacon.*

• *Add some fresh veggies halfway through for a little color.*

QUESADILLA

There are so many variations of a quesadilla. Don't be afraid to play around with this one. Swap ingredients or add in some new ones. You can't mess this one up.

SERVES 4

INSTRUCTIONS

1. Prep 4 sheets of foil with nonstick spray.

2. Place 1 tortilla on each sheet of foil. Top with cheese and any additional toppings you want.

3. Fold over the tortilla and then seal the packet. Place on warm coals and heat 10–15 minutes until heated through.

INGREDIENTS

4 **flour tortillas**

1 cup **cheese**

OPTIONAL ADD-INS

chicken, cooked

steak, cooked

bacon

chopped **bell peppers**

chopped **onions**

TIP
• *Try topping your quesadillas with fresh pico de gallo or guacamole from Harmons for a great additional flavor.*

TIN FOIL PIZZA

These pizza flatbreads are fun to make for the entire family. Create a pizza topping bar and let everyone get creative.

SERVES 4

INSTRUCTIONS

1. Prep 4 sheets of foil with nonstick spray.

2. Spoon 2–3 tablespoons of sauce onto the center of each piece of flatbread. Add mozzarella and any additional toppings you desire.

3. Fold foil over and seal each one. Place on warm coals and bake 10–15 minutes until heated through.

INGREDIENTS

4 pieces **flatbread**

1 cup of your favorite **pizza sauce**

1 cup **mozzarella cheese**

TOPPINGS

pepperoni

peppers

onions

olives

pineapple

Canadian bacon

TIP
• *Use leftover sauce for dipping.*

SIDES

A good side dish can go a long way. Try one of these tried-and-true favorites to add to your meal.

CHEESY BACON **POTATOES**

This side dish is great in a foil packet or cooked in a Dutch oven.

SERVES 4

INSTRUCTIONS

1. Create 4 rectangles of heavy-duty foil. Spray them with cooking spray.

2. Stir the first 6 ingredients together in a large bowl. Divide evenly among the foil sheets. Sprinkle ¼ cup of cheese over each one.

3. Fold up the sides to create your packet.

4. Place your packets onto prepared coals. Cook for 1 hour or until the potatoes are soft, making sure to turn a few times for even cooking.

INGREDIENTS

8 slices **bacon**, cooked and chopped

3 large **potatoes**, cubed

½ cup finely diced **onions**

½ tsp. **salt**

¼ tsp. **pepper**

¼ cup **butter**, melted

1 cup **cheddar cheese**, divided

SMOTHERED FRENCH FRIES

These cheese fries are the ultimate camping comfort food. We like to eat them all on their own or on the side with hot dogs!

SERVES 4

INSTRUCTIONS

1. Create a large rectangle out of heavy-duty foil. Mist with cooking spray.

2. Place the french fries in the middle of your prepared packet. Season with salt.

3. Top with cheese and chilies, if using. Fold up the edges of the foil and seal tightly.

4. Place on prepared coals. Cook 10–15 minutes or until heated through.

INGREDIENTS

1 pkg. **frozen french fries**

salt, to taste

½ cup shredded **cheddar cheese**

½ cup shredded **pepper jack cheese**

1 can diced **green chilies** (optional)

TIPS

•*Not a fan of pepper jack cheese? Use more cheddar cheese instead.*

• *Top with crumbled bacon for added flavor.*

JALAPEÑO POPPERS

These poppers make a great appetizer for a crowd.

SERVES 4

INSTRUCTIONS

1. Mist 2 sheets of foil with nonstick spray. Set aside.

2. Combine cream cheese, parmesan cheese, garlic powder, cheddar cheese, and bacon in a bowl. Stir until fully combined.

3. Slice jalapeños in half lengthwise. Remove the seeds and membrane with a spoon.

4. Fill each half with a heaping amount of the cream cheese mixture. Place half of the jalapeños on each piece of foil. Fold up the edges, sealing carefully.

5. Place on a grate over the fire and cook for 30 minutes or until the peppers are tender.

INGREDIENTS

4 oz. **cream cheese**

2 Tbsp. grated **parmesan cheese**

½ tsp. **garlic powder**

¾ cup shredded **cheddar cheese**

4 slices **bacon**, cooked and crumbled

8 **jalapeños**

TIP
• *Keep a close eye on the fire to make sure it doesn't get too big or go out.*

ROSEMARY POTATOES

These potatoes pair well with almost any main dish. Try them with the Parmesan Chicken Dinner on page 32.

SERVES 4

INSTRUCTIONS

1. Whisk together the olive oil, garlic, rosemary, and Dijon mustard. Toss your cubed potatoes in the mixture. Season with salt and pepper, to taste.

2. Prepare a large sheet of foil by misting with cooking spray. Pour potato mixture in the center of the foil. Fold up the edges, sealing tightly.

3. Cook on prepared coals for 1 hour or until potatoes are tender.

INGREDIENTS

2 Tbsp. **olive oil**

2 cloves **garlic**

2 tsp. chopped **rosemary**

½ tsp. **Dijon mustard**

1 lb. cubed **red potatoes**

salt and **pepper**, to taste

ROASTED BROCCOLI **AND** CHEESE

This roasted broccoli dish is simple to whip up and the perfect side to any meal.

SERVES 4

INSTRUCTIONS

1. Prepare 2 sheets of foil and mist with cooking spray.
2. Whisk together the lemon juice, olive oil, garlic powder, and salt and pepper. Toss your broccoli in the mixture and divided between the foil sheets. Fold up the edges sealing tightly.
3. Cook on warm coals 15 minutes, turning frequently.
4. Sprinkle with parmesan cheese and serve.

INGREDIENTS

2 Tbsp. **lemon juice**

2 Tbsp. **olive oil**

¼ tsp. **garlic powder**

salt and **pepper**, to taste

3 cups chopped **broccoli**

½ cup **parmesan cheese**

VEGGIE PACKETS

Add some vegetables into your menu with these easy Veggie Packets.

SERVES 4

INSTRUCTIONS

1. Whisk together the olive oil, garlic, and salt and pepper.

2. Toss your veggies in the olive oil mixture. Divide between four foil sheets. Fold up the edges and seal tightly.

3. Cook over warmed coals for 30 minutes or until vegetables are tender.

INGREDIENTS

3 Tbsp. **olive oil**

1 clove **garlic**

salt and **pepper**, to taste

1 **yellow squash**, sliced

1 **zucchini**, sliced

¼ cup sliced **carrots**

½ cup **mushrooms**

½ cup sliced **onion**

TIP
• *This recipe is very forgiving, so add or take out any veggies you choose.*

CHEESY GARLIC BREAD

Cheesy garlic bread is a must with any pasta or pizza dish. Did you know you can make it over the fire?

SERVES 8–10

INSTRUCTIONS

1. Cut your bread into thick slices. Place the loaf in the center of a sheet of heavy-duty foil.

2. Mix together the remaining ingredients and spread onto each slice. Wrap foil tightly around the loaf and cook on heated coals 10 minutes, turning halfway through.

INGREDIENTS

1 loaf **French bread**

¼ cup fresh grated **parmesan cheese**

½ cup **butter**, softened

1½ Tbsp. **garlic powder**

1 tsp. **dried parsley**

ONION BREAD

This bread was served as a Sunday dinner side in my husband's family for years. It's simple to make and unbelievably delicious.

SERVES 12–16

INSTRUCTIONS

1. Set a large sheet of foil on a clean surface.

2. Place your sliced loaf of bread in the middle. Spread the melted butter on each piece of bread. Sprinkle the green onions over the top letting pieces fall into the crevices. Wrap the foil around the bread and seal tightly.

3. Cook on warm coals 15–20 minutes or until slightly toasted and warmed through. Make sure to turn tin foil packet frequently.

INGREDIENTS

1 loaf **French bread**, sliced

½ cup **butter**, melted

¼–½ cup sliced **green onions**

DESSERTS

End your meal or day on a sweet note. These fun dishes
are new ways to enjoy dessert over the open flame!

APPLE CRISP

This simple apple crisp is a great way to add a little sweetness to your trip.

SERVES 2

INSTRUCTIONS

1. Prepare 2 foil packets by misting with cooking spray.
2. Whisk together the sugar, flour, cinnamon, and nutmeg. Toss the apples in mixture. Divide between your 2 packets.
3. Combine the oats, brown sugar, baking powder, baking soda, and butter in a small bowl. Pour over your apple mixture.
4. Seal your packets and place on the grate over your heated coals. Cook 15–20 minutes or until cooked through.

INGREDIENTS

¼ cup **sugar**

¾ cup **flour**

¼ tsp. **cinnamon**

1 pinch of **nutmeg**

3 **Granny Smith apples**, diced

½ cup **quick oats**

¼ cup **brown sugar**

⅛ tsp. **baking powder**

⅛ tsp. **baking soda**

¼ cup **butter**, melted

MONKEY BREAD

This sweet treat uses canned rolls and is perfect as breakfast or dessert! It's a family favorite that we make outdoors or back at home.

SERVES 2-4

INSTRUCTIONS

1. Prepare 2 tin foil sheets by spraying with nonstick cooking spray. Set aside.

2. Stir together the sugar with the cinnamon. Cut each biscuit into 4 pieces and roll into your cinnamon mixture. Divide biscuit pieces between your 2 packets.

3. Cut the butter into small cubes. Sprinkle evenly between the two servings. Sprinkle with brown sugar and seal tightly by folding up the edges.

4. Cook on a grate over hot coals 20 minutes or until the biscuits are cooked through. Make sure to turn frequently for even cooking.

INGREDIENTS

¼ cup **sugar**

1 tsp. **cinnamon**

1 can **biscuits**

4 Tbsp. **butter**

¼ cup **brown sugar**

STUFFED APPLES

The easier version of apple pie. These stuffed apples soften while cooking over the fire, leaving you with a new twist on a classic dessert.

SERVES 2

INSTRUCTIONS

1. Mist 2 sheets of heavy-duty foil with cooking spray.

2. Whisk together the brown sugar, cinnamon, and vanilla.

3. Place one apple on each tin foil sheet. Divide the sugar mixture and stuff it into the 2 apples. Top with 1 tablespoon butter each.

4. Wrap tightly in foil. Cook on the warmed coals 10 minutes or until each apple is soft.

INGREDIENTS

2 Tbsp. **brown sugar**

½ tsp. **cinnamon**

¼ tsp. **vanilla extract**

2 **apples**, cored

2 Tbsp. **butter**, divided

TIPS

• *Use Granny Smith or a more tart apple to help contrast the flavors.*

• *A melon baller makes it simple to core the apple.*

• *Top with whipped cream or vanilla ice cream for extra flair.*

GRILLED PINEAPPLE CAKE

This is the cheat version of a pineapple upside down cake. Easy to make and even easier to watch disappear.

SERVES 6

INSTRUCTIONS

1. Prep 6 foil packets with nonstick cooking spray.

2. Spread 2 tablespoons of brown sugar in the middle of each sheet of foil. Top with 1 tablespoon of butter.

3. Place 1 ring of pineapple (and cherry, if using) on top of sugar. Add a pound cake to each and cover tightly with foil.

4. Cook on the outer coals or over a grate, sugar-side down, for 10 minutes, flipping once halfway through.

INGREDIENTS

¾ cup **brown sugar**, divided

6 Tbsp. **butter**, divided

1 small can **pineapple rings**

cherries (optional)

6 small **pound cakes**

CHEAT FRUIT COBBLER

This is one of the most popular recipes on my site. Originally we made this in a Dutch oven but swapped to individual-sized ones for a fun spin.

SERVES 8–10

INSTRUCTIONS

1. Stir together the cake mix, sprite, and cinnamon. Divide between two 9-inch foil dishes.

2. Pour 1 can of drained peaches into each batter-filled dish. Cover with heavy-duty foil and place on a grate over hot coals. Cook 30 minutes or until a toothpick comes out clean.

INGREDIENTS

1 box **yellow cake mix**

1 can **sprite**

¾ tsp. **cinnamon**

2 (30-oz.) cans **peaches**, drained

POUND CAKE **AND** BERRIES

Another simple dessert that is perfect for your outdoor adventures!

SERVES 6

INSTRUCTIONS

1. Prepare 5 sheets of foil with nonstick spray.
2. Spread softened butter on each side of a slice of the pound cake slices. Place buttered slices in the center of each foil packet and seal tightly.
3. Cook on a grate over heated coals 3 minutes on each side.
4. Combine berries and sugar in a bowl. Divide between your heated cakes. Top with whipped cream and enjoy!

INGREDIENTS

butter, softened

1 **pound cake**, sliced thickly

2 cups **mixed berries** of your choice

2 Tbsp. **sugar**

whipped cream (optional)

S'MORE QUESADILLA

A twist on the classic s'more dessert!

SERVES 4

INSTRUCTIONS

1. Spread 1–2 tablespoons Nutella on half of each tortilla. Sprinkle with either marshmallows or banana slices (or both!). Fold in half, creating a half circle. Wrap tightly in foil and heat over warm coals until toasted, turning frequently.

INGREDIENTS

¼–½ cup **Nutella** or **chocolate spread**, divided

4 (8-inch) **tortillas**

½ cup **mini marshmallows**

½ cup **banana** slices

CINNAMON SUGAR BANANAS

Grilled bananas are a treat you should try at least once in your life. A healthier dessert that's perfect to share.

SERVES 2

INSTRUCTIONS

1. Spray 2 sheets of foil with nonstick spray.

2. Stir sugar and cinnamon together.

3. Slice each banana peel lengthwise. Gently open the peel, making sure to keep it intact, and slice your banana. Sprinkle with cinnamon and sugar mixture and drizzle with honey.

4. Wrap in foil and cook 5 minutes or until warm.

INGREDIENTS

3 Tbsp. **sugar**

1½ tsp. **cinnamon**

3 large **bananas**, unpeeled

honey, to taste

INDEX

INDEX

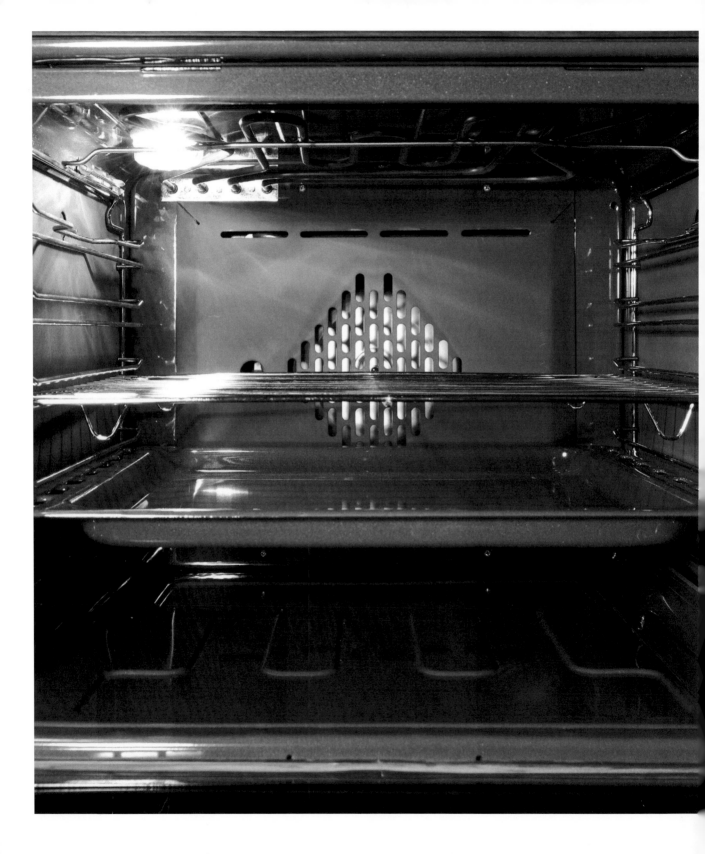

NOTES

NOTES

NOTES

COOKING MEASUREMENT EQUIVALENTS

CUPS	TABLESPOONS	FLUID OUNCES
⅛ cup	2 Tbsp.	1 fl. oz.
¼ cup	4 Tbsp.	2 fl. oz.
⅓ cup	5 Tbsp. + 1 tsp.	
½ cup	8 Tbsp.	4 fl. oz.
⅔ cup	10 Tbsp. + 2 tsp.	
¾ cup	12 Tbsp.	6 fl. oz.
1 cup	16 Tbsp.	8 fl. oz.

CUPS	FLUID OUNCES	PINTS/QUARTS/GALLONS
1 cup	8 fl. oz.	½ pint
2 cups	16 fl. oz.	1 pint = ½ quart
3 cups	24 fl. oz.	1½ pints
4 cups	32 fl. oz.	2 pints = 1 quart
8 cups	64 fl. oz.	2 quarts = ½ gallon
16 cups	128 fl. oz.	4 quarts = 1 gallon

Other Helpful Equivalents

1 Tbsp.	3 tsp.
8 oz.	½ lb.
16 oz.	1 lb.

METRIC MEASUREMENT EQUIVALENTS

Approximate Weight Equivalents

OUNCES	POUNDS	GRAMS
4 oz.	¼ lb.	113 g
5 oz.		142 g
6 oz.		170 g
8 oz.	½ lb.	227 g
9 oz.		255 g
12 oz.	¾ lb.	340 g
16 oz.	1 lb.	454 g

Approximate Volume Equivalents

CUPS	US FLUID OUNCES	MILLILITERS
⅛ cup	1 fl. oz.	30 ml
¼ cup	2 fl. oz.	59 ml
½ cup	4 fl. oz.	118 ml
¾ cup	6 fl. oz.	177 ml
1 cup	8 fl. oz.	237 ml

Other Helpful Equivalents

½ tsp.	2½ ml
1 tsp.	5 ml
1 Tbsp.	15 ml

ABOUT THE AUTHOR

JESSECA HALLOWS is the recipe developer and photographer behind the popular website *One Sweet Appetite*. Her passion for food has driven her to create beautiful and tasty meals that the whole family will enjoy. Her work has been featured in online magazines as well as numerous news and media outlets. She lives and works near Salt Lake City, Utah, creating recipes for her site as well as major brands, including Kraft, Campbell's, Ghirardelli, and OXO.

SCAN to visit

WWW.ONESWEETAPPETITE.COM